Other books by Mike Magee, MD

Positive Doctors in America

The Best Medicine

Positive Leadership

The New Face of Aging

The Book of Choices

Order information:
1-800-774-3313
www.positiveprofiles.com

All

Available

Boats

All Available Boats

The Evacuation of Manhattan Island on September 11, 2001

Mike Magee, MD

Editor

SPENCER BOOKS / NEW YORK

Library of Congress Cataloging-in-Publication Data.

Magee, Mike

All Available Boats/Mike Magee, MD

144 p. 20.5cm x 20.5 cm
1. Magee, Mike
2. Photography, Journalistic
3. Leadership

I. Magee, Mike
II. Title
BF637.L4   2002   158.4-dc20
ISBN 1-889793-11-6

Printed in Canada
First printing October 2002

EDITOR
Mike Magee, MD

ART AND DESIGN
Mitchell Magee

COPY EDITORS
Michael Magee, Jr.
Richard Stepler

WRITERS
Norman Brouwer
Steven H. Jaffe
Robin K. Levinson
Laura Muha

PHOTOGRAPHERS
Andrew Garn
Carolina Salguero
Neil Selkirk
Greg Semendinger

RESEARCH ASSISTANTS
Jamie Dean
Allison Fashek
Jack Petzko
Shelley Preston

**Special thanks to the
South Street Seaport Museum for access
to their stories and images produced by
David Tarnow for their exhibit,
All Available Boats:
Harbor Voices & Images, 9.11.01
and Eneida Clarke for skillful coordination of this project.**

to the brave men and women
who lost their lives
on September 11, 2001

Contents

Peter Neill
Prologue

"All available boats!" The emergency message crackled across the marine radios of New York harbor's commercial fleet on the morning of September 11, 2001, summoning the boats and their crews to abandon their usual duties and respond to extraordinary circumstances. At the South Street Seaport Museum, we witnessed firsthand the stream of refugees from the World Trade Center, blinded and bedraggled, fleeing the collapse of the twin towers and the clouds of debris.

But as the astonishing photographs and stories in this book so dramatically depict, something quite different was happening on the other side of Manhattan, just six blocks away. The thousands of workers and residents of the World Trade Center and the surrounding area including the World Financial Center and Battery Park City were inundated with ash and debris – and had nowhere to turn.

What followed is a relatively unsung part of the city's response to the catastrophe. Ferries, tugboats, private vessels – even historic ships – became the agents of rescue. The bulkheads of the Hudson River esplanade became the awkward, but essential loading ramps for thousands of people fleeing across the harbor to Staten Island and New Jersey. The U.S. Coast Guard quickly enlisted, on the spur of the moment, civilian harbor pilots and tugboat captains to manage a remarkably efficient waterborne evacuation and help bring in rescue personnel and supplies. It was a heroic effort in the tradition of Dunkirk and other mythic movements by sea. And it was yet another demonstration of the competence and dedication of the New York maritime community.

In Mike Magee's beautifully crafted book – and in the exhibit recently opened in the South Street Seaport Museum's Port Life Gallery – are presented the portraits and stories of some of the maritime heroes of September 11. Nothing can equal what they saw or what they did. But this book and the exhibit tie the reader and the viewer to the people and the place on that special day. As a city, and as a nation, we have been wounded. But more importantly, we have transcended the immediate consequences of the attack with a palpable spirit of humanity, collaboration and resolve. That, too, is measurable through the efforts of those portrayed here. You can see the humanity in their faces. You can feel the spirit in their words. You can hear the resolve in their voices.

Peter Neill is the president of the South Street Seaport Museum in New York City.

Norman Brouwer
A New View From the Harbor – September 11

Some on the Harbor that morning witnessed the event unfolding from its first moments. Patrick Harris, captain and owner of the charter sailing yacht *Ventura*, was out on the deck of his boat in the North Cove Marina of Battery Park City, virtually in the shadow of the World Trade Center. He heard the loud engine of an aircraft and looked up just as the plane went into the north face of the north tower. For an instant there was a hole in the shape of the plane. Then the explosion came. The fireball erupted outward, but a moment later it seemed to be drawn back into the building.

Captain Frank Peters on the bridge of the ferry *John F. Kennedy* bound for Manhattan could only see the south face of the towers. He saw the fireball of an explosion over the Battery, which he thought must be a helicopter collision. He immediately notified the Coast Guard Vessel Traffic Service Center in Fort Wadsworth, Staten Island. The Center said they had also seen the explosion. Shortly after this Captain Peters contacted them again to say there was smoke indicating that the north tower of the World Trade Center was involved. Still believing the area affected by the incident would be limited and safely to the north, he went on into his slip east of Battery Park to discharge vehicles and passengers and load for the return trip to Staten

Island. Coast Guard Station New York on the shore of Staten Island facing Manhattan dispatched three high-speed boats operated by Petty Officers 1st Class Robin Shipley, Ken Walberg and Bill Simpson. Their instructions were to create a security zone from north of the World Trade Center to the entrance to the East River, and search for wreckage or survivors in the water from what was still believed to be an accidental plane crash into a tall building.

Marine Company 1, the City fireboat station on the west side of Manhattan, was located in the Gansevoort district two miles north of the World Trade Center. The men on duty heard the plane crash into the north tower, but thought it was a loud noise in a nearby construction site. Soon afterward the alarm came in for a fire at the Trade Center. Captain Ed Metcalf, on his second day with the Company, got the fireboat *John D. McKean* manned and underway. By the time they got to Battery Park City opposite the foot of Liberty Street the first injured people were arriving at the shore. Captain Metcalf gave the crew instructions to prepare the boat to serve as a staging area, and then headed inland to find the Fire Department command center.

When the second airplane hit the south tower the ferry *John F. Kennedy* was still in the slip loading vehicles and passengers. Captain Peters was startled by the noise of the plane, which seemed to be buzzing his pilothouse, but could not see where it went. Captain James Parese on the ferry *Samuel I. Newhouse*, which was now approaching Manhattan, saw the crash and immediately reported it over the radio. The Coast Guard boat crews, now off Lower Manhattan, watched in horror as the plane banked into its final turn and went straight into the building. The *Kennedy* now began getting passengers who simply wanted to escape whatever was happening. Captain Parese on the

Newhouse radioed Staten Island that he was not going to land his passengers in Manhattan. Already close to the end of his run, he continued past the Manhattan slips and into Buttermilk Channel, heading south between Governors Island and Brooklyn.

In an instant, the whole situation had gone through a dramatic change. What had been generally thought to be a tragic accident was now clearly an attack of as yet unknown magnitude, on the City of New York and, it would soon be learned, Washington, D.C. as well. The Coast Guard broadcast the order shutting down the Port and dispatched vessels to guard all approaches. The City shut down the subways and closed all bridges and tunnels to other than emergency vehicles.

Captain Andy McGovern of the Sandy Hook Pilots was in his car on the Belt Parkway, heading for a meeting on harbor safety that had originally been scheduled for 9:00 A.M. in the World Trade Center. Seeing the towers burning, he diverted to the Coast Guard Vessel Traffic Service Center on Staten Island to assist in coordinating operations. The Coast Guard now realized the magnitude of the evacuation that would be taking place and the number of boats it would involve. Lieutenant Mike Day, Coast Guard chief of the waterways oversight branch for New York, discussed with McGovern the need for a command center at the site. McGovern phoned the Sandy Hook Pilots' base on Staten Island and arranged to have the pilot vessel *New York* prepared to serve in this capacity. The *New York* would arrive in Manhattan, ready for operation, around 10:45.

The crew of the fireboat *McKean* had seen the second crash close at hand. The number of injured arriving at the shore increased, and more and more people began showing up who just wanted to get off Manhattan by any means available. Firemen brought injured people who

required assistance, and then went back to help others.

New York Waterways had a number of small commuter ferries operating on the Hudson River the morning of September 11. The Imperatore Family, pioneers in the revival of New York City commuting by water, had built up a fleet of twenty-four boats, twenty-three of which were in service that day. The president of New York Waterways, Arthur Imperatore, Jr., was about to leave for his office when the first crash was reported on Channel 2, the only television channel still on the air since the antenna used by all the other channels had been on the first tower hit. By the time he was on River Road on the way to the company's headquarters in Weehawken both towers were burning. In Weehawken he ordered all passenger operations into Manhattan shut down and directed boats to proceed to Lower Manhattan. Ferries needing crews were manned by licensed captains among the shore staff, and anyone else available in the maintenance shops and administrative offices. In ten minutes Arthur Imperatore was also on one of the Company's boats heading down the Hudson. He was five minutes out of Weehawken when the south tower of the World Trade Center collapsed.

The fall of the tower destroyed Police and Fire Department command centers that had been set up at the World Trade Center and large numbers of fire trucks and other emergency vehicles in the nearby streets. The area affected extended across West Street into the World Financial Center. Concerned firefighter Tom Sullivan from the fireboat *McKean* had just gone inland to look for Captain Metcalf when he heard the thunderous roar and was engulfed in the cloud. He managed to escape, crawling in complete darkness, in a rain of smaller debris. Captain Metcalf was found under larger debris and rushed to a hospital in Brooklyn, but was back on duty a few hours later.

Marine Division Supervisor Captain Al Fuentes was

less fortunate, but lucky to be alive. He had been trapped under wreckage at a command center, severely injured, but still able to use his radio. The fireboat *Smoke 2* had been in the East River preparing to go into the yard for overhaul. Rounding the Battery on their way to the scene they heard Captain Fuentes reporting his location. They docked at North Cove and sent men inland to find him, through the devastated Palm Court of the World Financial Center with its now partially shattered arched glass skylight. The men had to break through a ground floor window to get into the debris field in West Street, where they located Captain Fuentes, evacuating him to the river by the same route. They decided to take him over to Jersey City, where the flashing lights of emergency vehicles could now be seen.

Ken Peterson, Port Captain and Safety Engineer with Reinauer Towing, had been on board the *Morgan Reinauer* in the Company's Staten Island yard in the middle of an inspection. He saw the crash of the second plane, and then the collapse of the first tower. Soon afterward the *Jill Reinauer* in Erie Basin, Brooklyn radioed that the Coast Guard was asking "all available boats" to proceed to the vicinity of Lower Manhattan. There were four Reinauer tugs in the yard. Peterson assembled the captains, telling them he had no idea what they would be getting involved in, and that their participation and that of their crews would be purely voluntary. The warehouse was opened up and lifejackets and other supplies were loaded on the boats, and they got under way for Manhattan. When he arrived off Governors Island, Peterson radioed the Coast Guard saying there were already twenty tugs on hand, and asking for permission to land at the Battery. In moments the Coast Guard came back with the go ahead. Peterson went on the radio to "all Reinauer boats, and all other boats, Let's go in!"

When the tugs brought their bows up to the Battery sea wall they were greeted by an incredible sight.

A crowd of people, many of them completely gray with the dust, were climbing over the railing trying to get to any boat that would take them off the island. The tugs tried to do anything they could to make it easier for the people and alleviate their panic and discomfort. Sheets and towels were used to try to clean people off. Drinking water and food were provided. Ken Peterson later estimated that the tugs evacuated over 4,000 people from the Battery in the course of four hours.

Every operator of work boats in the Harbor responded with one or more vessels. Moran, McAllister, Reinauer and K-Sea each had six or seven tugs involved. Two boats working with divers responded. Han-Padron Associates had a diver in the water at Pier 90 on the Hudson River. They shut down the operation and headed for Lower Manhattan with their 25-foot inboard. M. G. McLaren had one crew working at the Fulton Fish Market and another with a boat in the Harlem River. The boat sped to the Fish Market to pick up those men and joined in the effort to evacuate people from Battery Park City. Captain Pamela Hepburn's historic tug *Pegasus* was in Staten Island undergoing restoration. After being driven out of her loft near the Trade Center, she went to Pier 63 to pick up her motor whaleboat and began ferrying people over to Jersey City. The seventy-year-old fireboat *John J. Harvey* was at her berth at Pier 63, on the Hudson River near the foot of West 23rd Street. She had been retired by the City in 1995, but rescued from the scrap yard by a group of enthusiasts who had restored her to operating condition. Members of her volunteer crew were now assembling on board. Her engineer, Tim Ivory, was on the New Jersey side of the Hudson well north of where boats were crossing the river, but he managed to talk the owner of a small boat into ferrying him across. Once sufficient crew were on board, the *Harvey* got underway for Lower Manhattan.

Their initial involvement entailed evacuating people from Battery Park City to Pier 40. A second large City fireboat, the *Firefighter*, had arrived and was assisting the *McKean* in pumping water from the river to firemen inland. The hydrants and water mains on West Street had been destroyed, making the fireboats the only source of water in some areas. More pumping capacity was sorely needed, and the *John J. Harvey* was now recruited to provide it. Fortunately, in restoring the *Harvey* to operating condition, her crew had also rehabilitated her pumps in order to spray water into the air during harbor celebrations. The *Harvey* would remain at her post for the rest of that week. When she ran low on fuel it was provided by a drift collecting tug of the U. S. Army Corps of Engineers, whose entire fleet of boats based at Caven Point in south Jersey City had also responded.

By early afternoon fewer and fewer people were showing up at the shore of Lower Manhattan to be evacuated. In the days that followed, the full extent of the disaster would sink in. But on that day, some 300,000 New Yorkers would be evacuated from Manhattan island by their neighbors.

Part 1
The Captains

Ken Peterson:

Kenneth L. Peterson Jr, Port Captain,
Reinauer Transportation

As we were standing on our deck and watched the second tower collapse, we decided that we

needed to do something. At the same time one of our tugboats, the *Jill Reinauer*, called and said, "The Coast Guard's looking for assistance. Can we help?"

We had four tugboats at the Reinauer dock in Staten Island, and we decided that we would take all four up to Manhattan. We got all the captains together, myself and Bert Reinauer. We told them we didn't know what we were getting into, but we wanted to know if they would volunteer to take their crew and boat up to Manhattan. All four of the captains said, yes, they would go.

As we approached Governors Island, I radioed the Coast Guard on channel 13 and said, "There's 10 or 15 tugboats out here. I'm Ken Peterson from Reinauer, I have four more and Reinauer wants to know if we can get on the island." Within a few minutes, they acknowledged my transmission and said, "Reinauer, you have permission to get on the island."

I got on the radio and said, "Break, break, this is Kenny Peterson. All the Reinauer boats and anybody else, let's go and get the people." And that's when we got on the lower Battery wall of Manhattan, right by the Staten Island Ferry. At the same time the pilot boat New York was going up to North Cove marina. The *New York* was the central command for everyone on the waterborne community.

We needed somebody to organize and co-ordinate everything on shore. I took a couple of telephones and some VHF radios, nominated a few other people I knew, and we got on the island and started telling the tugboats where to go to pick up people. We put from 100 to 150 people on each boat.

All we did was ask people, "Where's home, where do you want to go?" The people who said that they'd lost their homes, we sent them over to Jersey City or to Staten Island, figuring that buses and taxis could get them to hotels or some place to stay. Jersey City was very helpful in pro-

viding taxis and bus services

A lot of the people who came down to the Battery were covered with soot and crying, shaking. We thought if we could wash some of the soot off their faces, off their hands, with bed sheets and towels we could make them more comfortable. We wanted to make them feel that somebody did care about what they had just seen or had gone through.

We got on the island about 11:30 a.m. on Tuesday and we stayed there until Friday night. We worked 24-hour shifts. Everybody worked very well together because New York is such a small harbor that a lot of us know each other. When I got on the radio at 21:05 Friday night, everyone has it in their log books that I said, "Okay guys, this is Kenny Peterson, to all the tugboats on the wall. We've been relieved by the National Guard and the Army Corps of Engineers." I got calls from every boat that was there, saying, "Thank you Kenny, I'll work with you anytime."

Huntley Gill:

The Coast Guard was asking every vessel in the harbor to "please go down to the Battery,

go down to Pier 11 on the East River, be careful of people in the water, and get people off the island of Manhattan." By the time we got to the Battery both towers had collapsed. Some people looked like they had just walked out of their offices and were perfectly fine. Others had this horrible dust that covered them from head to foot. It was clear that they were all very anxious and they wanted to get home. But there was no panic. Just a quiet sense of urgency that was interesting.

By the time I figured we had 150 people, which is twice what we like to carry, we headed toward Pier 40 at Houston Street. As we passed the two city fireboats, they called us on the radio and said, "This is [FDNY's fireboat] *McKean*. *John J. Harvey* get rid of your passengers as fast as you can. We don't have any hydrants, and we need your water." So we thought, good, that's what this boat was built for. When she was built in 1931, the *Harvey* was the largest and most powerful fireboat in history.

The hydrants had been lost because of the collapse of the towers, and we ended up feeding fire hoses that snaked inland from the promenade at Battery Park City to Ground Zero. The other two fireboats were pumping hard. Each of these big fireboats can probably supply about 20 fire engines so it's a lot of water. We pump the equivalent of two standard suburban swimming pools full of water a minute.

For the first two days everyone was just pitching in and doing what had to be done without instruction. There was no panic on anybody's part. It was a sense of determination, an understanding of the urgency, and there was a clarity that nobody should be sitting down.

Tim Ivory:

As we approached the waterfront as close as possible to the base of the towers, a lieutenant from

Marine 6 named Tom White yelled over to me, "Do your pumps work?" I gave him a thumbs up, because there's no sense yelling above the sound of the engines. He yelled back, "Can you take hoses?" I gave him a thumbs up again. As we got up closer and started to put lines out, he asked, "What do you need to make this work? " I said that we had about 300 gallons of fuel on board and that we could pump for about an hour. He got on the radio and said, "Harvey needs fuel, critical." Within 15 or 20 minutes an Army Corps of Engineers tug pulled up alongside to deliver fuel. It was awe inspiring.

We made our hose connections, and the water started to flow probably within half an hour after we tied up. Slowly more lines were brought to us and we would pump more water inland. At the peak we had three 3-inch lines and one 2-1/2 inch line.

Later in the second day our pumping detail was finished. They had restored the water mains, but they were reluctant to release us for fear of other problems. So while they didn't ask us to stay, they didn't exactly tell us we could leave, either. They did kind of mention that "if you're not doing anything or have nowhere else to be, we could use you here." It was the general consensus aboard the Harvey that we couldn't think of any place we'd rather be in the world.

Kimberely Gochberg:

Kimberely Gochberg, Intercollegiate Sailing Coach, U.S. Merchant Marine Academy

We were driving to work and just before we reached the main gates, the President announced that

it was a terrorist attack on the radio. One of our co-workers immediately started getting everybody organized into crews to man the academy's motorboats.

That morning, we drove our powerboats into the city. Because the Coast Guard had closed New York harbor to all traffic, we carried letters from the admiral of the academy saying that we were part of the relief effort so they would let us through.

When we reached the South Street Seaport area, it was engulfed in black smoke from the fires. We could also see people covered by gray ash walking across the bridges. The only way to get around seemed to be by foot or by powerboat.

First, we carried doctors from the South Street Seaport to a triage area at North Cove that was closer to the disaster site. After we transported the doctors, we went to the Brooklyn Navy Yard where teams of firefighters were waiting for us. We took them to North Cove, too.

The thing I remember about North Cove is all the gray ash, pulverized concrete and documents and paper that had fallen from the Trade Center that covered the boats docked there. Also, we could see that the tugboats at the Battery that were evacuating people were also covered with what looked like three inches of ash, dust and debris. You could actually see the ash flakes just dropping from the sky. People were inhaling the ash, and it was obviously a danger. A lot of people wearing masks, and we were all issued masks to use.

After the first day we were put on a rotation schedule and basically worked for about two weeks running boats in and out and helping firemen get to where they needed to go. We just asked them where they needed to go, and we drove them there. There were no more questions.

A lot of us worked throughout the night, and we were basically running nonstop. I was running a hard-bottom inflatable, which was able to carry about six firemen. The firemen were working 24-hour shifts, so we were taking in fresh firemen and taking out exhausted men.

I made sure that every time a fireman got on or off the boat we would thank them for what they were doing, and they would in return thank us for the ride. Transportation by powerboat was so much faster than any other kind of transportation at that time.

Tom Sullivan:

The crew of Marine 1, FDNY fireboat *John D. McKean* (top, left to right): Robert Petersen and Joseph Stark: (bottom, left to right):Timothy Goss, James Campanelli, Thomas Sullivan, and Thomas Tracy

That morning we jumped on the boat and were down at the Trade Towers within about five

minutes. As we nosed into the pier we heard the roar of another plane. It sounded like you were at the airport and a plane was taking off, that's how thunderous the sound was.

We looked to our right and saw another plane barreling in, descending right over the Statue of Liberty. As the plane was descending, it was accelerating and you could hear the engines revving. We thought he was trying to get a closer look at the fire, but we didn't really know what he was doing. At the last minute he tipped his wings and went right into the south side of Tower 2. Once we saw that we knew it was a terrorist act.

As we tied up to the bulkhead, people were fleeing from the area. Some were burnt or cut up, some were helping each other or carrying other people. There were New York Waterway ferries taking people over to Jersey. We got off the McKean and started to help the people who were injured the worst. Ed Metcalf, our captain, went to the command post to get orders from the fire chiefs in case we had to start stretching hoses into the Trade Towers to supply them with water.

After we were secured to the sea wall, people started to jump onto our boat. It was low tide so they had to jump down about 10 feet off a concrete wall. But they weren't waiting for assistance so some of them broke their legs when they hit our deck.

People were just diving onto the boat. We were trying to catch them, trying to help them get on. Mothers and nannies with infants in their arms were dropping the children down to us. At one point we had four or five of them wrapped in little blankets, and we put them in bunks down in the crew quarters. I put four of the babies in one bunk, like little peanuts lined up in a row. And then we helped the mothers and nannies down. At the same time two women who had jumped missed the boat and ended up going into the water. We pulled one of them out pretty quickly. But

the other woman was hanging onto the bow of the boat and was getting pushed against the bulkhead. It was ebb tide--the current was running out to sea--and the boat was facing north so the tide was pushing against the bow, and it was a strong current.

So [Marine 1 crewmember] Greg Woods dove into the water. Greg's second job is a lifeguard. He grabbed the woman around the waist and held her up. But she had completely given up; she had no energy left. We dropped the Jacob's ladder over the side. Being near the bow , the ladder was a little short, and the woman could barely reach it. Finally, she managed to get one hand on the ladder but she couldn't get the other hand up because she just didn't have the energy. Greg dove underneath her and pushed her up until she was able to get both hands on the ladder.

I was hanging over the side of the boat telling her, "Take a couple of seconds, take a break, take a deep breath, we're gonna make one more move and get you up on this ladder." Then Greg gave her another boost, and she got her knee up on the ladder. It was like slow motion: She only had to go about eight to 10 feet in all to reach the deck of the boat. Finally, she got her whole body on the ladder, and then we reached down and grabbed her and pulled her in.

Patrick Harris:

Patrick Harris, Captian of the *Ventura*, a 63 foot charter boat

We were sitting there talking when Jack suddenly shouted, Look! I turned and just caught the tail of

an airplane disappearing into the north tower. For a split second, it was completely silent, but suddenly there was a loud Whump! and a large balloon-shaped fireball erupted from the north side of the building and was sucked back within a second or two. Then all of the windows lit up like an arcade game, the entire floor from left to right.

When I called the Coast Guard, I simply could not bring myself to say that I saw a jet airplane fly over the WTC. So I said there had been a tremendous explosion at the WTC, over. The CG paused, then said they would inform the appropriate departments. I believe it was the first CG had heard of it.

Jack kept repeating over and over, "It was a jet, it was a jet."

Now people started coming out of the buildings around the plaza, several hundred people. We wanted to get a better look at what happened, so we went to the north side, to Vesey and West Street. We could see the outline of the plane, like a cookie cutter had punched the shape of an airplane through the center of the building. The street corner was jam packed with hundreds of people. Then someone yelled, "Here comes another one!" We saw another plane zoom into the other building. We saw the plane turn and enter and then heard the explosion. It took only a second or two. Then collectively, everyone began to scream and run. The incident had changed from an accident to an attack. My instinct was to return to the boat and get it out of there. I didn't feel fear, I felt like an observer. But I needed to get the boat out of there because it was my livelihood. I had to literally run and dodge people to get back.

When I got back to the boat, I saw my first mate, Josh, who was shouting, "Where's my family, where's my family?" And his wife, Amber, who was eight months pregnant and really big, was coming towards him. I said, get your wife onboard and let's get out of here. He said my family's at the WTC, my brothers are over there. So I started to get the boat ready and Josh went to get his brothers – they lived at Gateway Plaza – his twin brother and his other two brothers who are also twins.

Now the plaza was completely deserted and we had to get out. Two boats had already left, including the one next to us, which is lucky for us because the Ventura is 63 feet and we needed the maneuvering room. At that point, we had about eight people on the boat, Josh and his three brothers, and Amber.

I remember looking back at Amber sitting on the back seat of the boat. She was wearing a maternity dress, and I noticed that the lower part of her legs were covered with blood. She was due in about four weeks, and I thought she was going to have the baby right there. As it turned out, Amber and Josh just exited the subway to the south of the WTC, and were walking underneath the south tower when the second jet crashed. As they crossed the street, bodies and body parts were falling and splattering on the ground. So parts of other people were stuck to her legs. She was shaken up but she was okay. She was not giving birth.

As we started to leave North Cove, a police boat was approaching, so I called them. We went out into the river and we paused, where do we go: north or south? Then I thought that this is not an accident, it's an attack, things are going to be shut down here, so we should get fuel for the boat. So we went across the river to a fuel dock at a marina on the Morris Canal in Hoboken. There was no traffic to speak of in the harbor. It was still early but the marina staff had all left so there was no one available to pump fuel.

Someone said people were jumping off the seawall south of the WTC, you should go look for them. So that's exactly what we did: we went back across the river towards Manhattan.

The towers now were burning fiercely and you could see people jumping out of the buildings. They were mostly jumping from the south side of the south tower. And there were a lot of them, a lot of them. Two or three were in the air at any given time. Some of the people seemed to be small and light because the wind seemed to catch them and flip them like a leaf but most people just plummeted straight down. I had everyone on the boat put on life jackets.

The wind was north by northwest and the smoke was black and thick and pouring over Manhattan and over the East River.

Paul Amico:

I own Amico Ironworks, and I'm one of the main fabricators for New York Waterway. I Build the floating

docks, gangways and hinge systems for their ferry boats.

On the morning of September 11 I was about five miles west of the Hudson River near Giant Stadium. Coming over an overpass I saw the smoke from the World Trade Center. I immediately went back to my shop, which is only a mile and a half away, grabbed my marine radio, life jacket and headed straight for Jersey City to hop on a ferry. I knew that New York Waterway had to do an evacuation. I feel responsible for building their docks, and so I felt responsible for getting the people out of there safely.

I boarded one of our ferries in Jersey City. Halfway across the river, I saw the first tower fall. The ferry pulled through the cloud of smoke--we went in by radar. There were probably eight or nine ferries evacuating people from our terminal at North Cove in Battery Park City. I got off the ferry, spoke with one of the managers, and let him know that I had a radio, that I could communicate.

At that point the fire and the police department closed our dock at North Cove, so we had to move passengers out of another area. I grabbed my radio and walked north to Stuyvesant High School where they let us work. I then directed ferries in by radio to where we had hooked up what we call a "man overboard ladder" against the sea wall.

If we had injured people on board, mostly firemen, we immediately released the ladder and sent that boat back to Jersey. The ferry captains would call ahead to let them know to have ambulances ready. Then we'd bring in another boat. At one point we were loading three or four boats at a time.

When they closed the Stuyvesant High School area, I told the ferries that we were moving north to Pier 26, home of the Downtown Boathouse, a kayak club I belong to and where I knew we had enough water to get the ferries in. I opened the boathouse, got an acetylene torch, and I was able to cut the fences down so we could get the ferries in tight to the wall without having people climb over the fences.

Everyone did what they needed to do. No one had to tell anyone what to do. The mechanics who usually repair the boats hopped on boats to work as crew mates. The job of the staff of New York Waterway is to move people in and out of Manhattan and that's what they did. They didn't know if the buildings would fall on them, and they didn't know if there were more airplanes coming. The scariest part was when fighter jets were flying over Manhattan. We didn't know whose they were, and they were coming close to us.

Most people were orderly getting on and off the boats. There was a tremendous amount of fear. The difficult part was if there were groups of people together and they were separated. For example, a three-year-old child wound up on one boat, the parents wound up on another and they went to two different locations. The ferry captains radioed each other and were able to get them back together.

I only had time to act, I didn't have time to react. It took me a few days to react. The following weekend after working about 50 hours straight, I was installing a ferry terminal directly across from the World Trade Center. To drive the pilings, you line them up with a tall building to see if they're straight. And I turned around to see if the pilings were straight by looking at the World Trade Center like I would usually do. Of course, the towers were gone. And I burst out in tears.

Jack Akerman:

Jack Akerman, Sandy Hook Harbor Pilot

On the morning of September 11, I was in my office on Staten Island when I was notified by one

of my crew members that smoke was coming from the north tower of the World Trade Center. One of our pilots, Andy McGovern, had also heard it on the news and went directly to the Coast Guard Vessel Traffic Service Center, which is also on Staten Island. He called our office and said that the Coast Guard was looking for a platform for an on-scene commander to help with the evacuation of downtown Manhattan.

So we got our four vessels under way to the Battery. When we got there it was encouraging and amazing to see the amount of maritime traffic. There were tug boats, municipal tankers, water taxis, ferries, an unimaginable assortment of water craft to help in the evacuation.

We set up station just off the Battery. Our job was to direct the boats to different areas, to move resources around the tip of the Battery, from South Street Seaport on the East River up to the World Financial Center on the Hudson. We also put people ashore to direct evacuees toward the boats. When the boats contacted us we got the name, the size, the draft, how many people they thought they could carry. That kind of information. And then we'd be able to disperse them throughout the lower part of Manhattan. At any given time, Battery Park was ringed by 10 or 12 boats waiting for people to come on board. After the boats were loaded, they'd ask people where they wanted to go and they'd take them there.

One of the advantages the maritime industry people have over the Coast Guard is that we know most of the vessels that work in the harbor because we've been here for our whole lives. We know the size and capabilities of the vessels, so we understand where they can fit and where they can't fit. Knowing the height of the tug and how high its deck was, you could send it to a place where people could step into the boat instead of having to climb into it. So having the pilots out there was really an advantage because we were able to deploy the boats in a pretty effi-

cient fashion.

Later that evening, Hank Mahlmann, one of our pilots who was ashore, ran into a fireman who told him they needed drinking water. I'm not actually sure to this day sure how it happened, but we found out there was water available in Jersey City. So we sent a couple of boats over to pick up a supply of these three-gallon water-cooler-size bottles. Somebody must have commandeered a truckload of them because they just kept coming across the river. Well, one thing led to another and next thing we were bringing Jersey City firemen and police over to help out.

While we were docked at North Cove Marina in Battery Park City, firemen asked if they could get fuel from us--their fire trucks were starting to run out. We were sitting on top of 40,000 gallons of diesel. So we took some of the water bottles and started filling them with fuel and somebody with a pickup truck drove around to the fire trucks and fueled them up. All night long this shuttle of food, water and personnel kept coming over from New Jersey. It was truly amazing to watch the spirit of these people as they came over.

By the time we got home, we were just exhausted. It was definitely more emotional than it was physical. I remember one day I was at Ground Zero, and it looked like ants on a hill: Firemen, police, iron workers and rescue workers were digging through the pile with buckets. I just wanted somebody to yell "Cut!" It looked like a movie, like it couldn't really be happening. But it was.

James Parese:

James Parese, Captain of the Staten Island Ferry, *Samuel I. Newhouse*

On the morning of September 11, we were leaving the St. George dock in Staten Island at approx-

imately 8:48, heading north for Manhattan with our usual load of passengers. When we left the ferry slip we noticed the smoke coming from the first building. As we were northbound we watched the fire through binoculars. When we were just off Governors Island we noticed the second plane coming overhead. We watched how it just glided into the second building. At that point we knew it was no accident. At first, we couldn't believe it; it almost looked like a movie. The plane just disappeared into the building. We heard a muffled explosion and we saw a big red ball of flames come out of the side of the building.

At that point I radioed my office, the Coast Guard and a police boat, notifying them of what we had just witnessed and that we didn't think it was a good idea to put a couple of thousand people onshore in Manhattan in that situation. The police boat told us to take the passengers back to Staten Island.

We got back safely and discharged our passengers. We were told that there was going to be an evacuation of Manhattan so we turned around and headed back north. I contacted our chief engineer: I wanted to know how fast I could make the boat run. He told me I could push it up over 800 rpm. So we got back to Manhattan fast.

When we were in the ship loading dock at [the Staten Island Ferry Terminal] Whitehall, we heard over the radio that the first building had fallen. We kept loading, and then we noticed this ash coming over us. We were pretty full, and there was a lull in the crowd so the crew was able to close the gates. I ordered the AC [assistant captain] to set up the radar, and we backed out. People were jumping from the aprons onto the boat, and they were jumping from the rack onto the boat. One guy jumped onto the hurricane deck, then slid down to the next deck and almost went into the water. Somebody asked him what he was trying to do. He said, "I'm jumping for my life." You couldn't deny him that. People were under the impression that Manhattan was being bombed.

As we were leaving, the boat filled with smoke. We headed southbound on radar because there was zero visibility. When I ran to the other side [the pilothouse on the other end of the ferry], I ran over the top and I had all white ash all over me. My eyes and lungs were burning from the smoke. There was dust all over the boat. People were crying, people were covered with dust and some people had no shoes. The mates and the deckhands were down on the passenger decks trying to calm everyone. As we got to the south end of Governors Island, we started coming out of the smoke and that's when everybody pretty much calmed down. We had at least 6,000 people on the boat, and after we left them on Staten Island we headed back to Manhattan.

The subways were down, and they closed the bridges. We were basically the only way out. Us and the smaller ferries, the police boats and the tugs. I couldn't believe the amount of tugs; there was a sea of tugboats coming from Staten Island heading for Manhattan.

We're under Coast Guard regulations on the ferry, and they require weekly and monthly drills. Every week we do a fire and boat drill, an emergency steering drill and an emergency anchor drill. So a lot of it becomes routine. It paid off because everybody did their job. The people we evacuated were thanking us, they were glad to see us. We've been getting letters telling us how happy they are that we were there.

During that day my biggest concern was the safety of the passengers, the vessel and my crew and making the right decisions at the right time. The main thing was to do what we do every day, but we had to do it right that day. Everyone pretty much did what they had to do. I think at those times it brings out the best in everybody.

Part 2
The Passengers

Lee Gruzen:

Lee Gruzen, Battery Park City Resident

I live on the edge of the Hudson River. Just before nine AM on September 11, I was ready

to go for a very full day and I had an elaborate schedule of events. They were all going to be in the neighborhood near the World Trade Center. As I was standing by the window there was a tremor, a series of tremors. Although they weren't loud, they were unusual. So I registered the time on the clock, because I thought, "This is something important." I looked out the window, which overlooks the promenade, and I could see people running. Two women looked at each other and said, "Oh, my God," and took off.

I'm told that everything got dark, but I don't remember black. I remember feeling like a primitive person when the sun is cut off in an eclipse, and you're just praying that the daylight is going to come back.

And then it got snow white as if it were a tremendous blizzard at the top of a mountain. You couldn't see more than an inch outside the window. But then it cleared. The breeze cleared it and it was like a miracle to see the sunlight coming back.

I didn't think about leaving at first, but then the second building collapsed and the same thing happened all over again. I thought now we have to get out of here. And the evacuation boats started to come into South Cove, which is beneath my window.

So I packed things very quickly. There were about nine people here, so I made peanut butter and jelly sandwiches for everybody. I got face cloths and made them wet and put them in little baggies for everybody.

There were a number of boats lined up under the window, mostly police boats. We went onto a boat that turned out to be a dive boat owned by a marine engineering company. I remember that men with big arms helped us aboard and everything was blue. I've since learned it was the tarp over the dive equipment and the boat had blue bumpers. But I just remember this bright blue and holding on and thinking, "Thank God the river's here, because if it weren't then this highway to safety wouldn't be there."

Then something extraordinary happened. The *Half Moon* sailed by. It was a replica of Henry Hudson's ship *Half Moon*, almost 400 years to the day Hudson originally entered New York harbor in it. It's very colorful. It looks a little like the Mayflower, only it's a Dutch boat. The uncanniness of its being there on that day, marking one of the major events in the history of the port of New York, was just extraordinary.

We went over to Exchange Place in Jersey City, straight across the river from where I live in Battery Park City, the closest point they could go to. The tide must have been out because the dock was very high. They took us off over the bow of the boat and had to pull us up. There weren't many people there, but they got us off the dock, and they had water for us. So I was grateful for that. This was probably about 11:15.

I have always felt more comfortable on the edge of rivers or on the edge of a bay. When I go away for the summer, I am never happy when I'm on the ocean. I've always felt safer on the edge of more benign water. My family and I have always lived on the edge of water. So I was thinking about the evacuation, about the fact that I always want to be near a place where I can get out by water.

Jacqui Gibbs:

Jacqueline "Jacqui" Gibbs, Vice President and Diversity Manager, JPMorgan Chase

At 8:46, when the first plane hit, I was stuck in the PATH train. Normally, I'm at the World Trade

Center by 8:45 and arrive at my desk at 9. But that day, my train leaving Scotch Plains was 15 minutes late.

We didn't know why the PATH had stopped until a guy on the train received an email or something saying a plane had hit one of the towers. We thought it was a fluke.

After 30 or 45 minutes, the train backed up and let us off at Christopher Street. I got out not knowing where I was. I'd been working in New York, as a vice president and diversity manager for JPMorgan Chase, for all of three months. I really didn't have a commuting buddy or any system other than going from the PATH train through the World Trade Center, then going the one block up to Chase.

I noticed Penny, a young lady I had conversed with briefly on the train. Her office was directly across from the World Trade Center. I knew that if I followed her, I'd find my building. We walked to a corner that would give us a good view of the World Trade Center. Both towers were in flames. We could see figures of people, jumping. When the building fell, I began to cry and think of all of the people lost in the collapse. We saw the fighter jets and the tanks coming through. It was like being in a war movie.

I latched on to Penny. I had never met this woman before in my life, and we were walking around the streets holding each other and crying.

My mind told me I needed to get home, so we just started walking with no clear destination. Then it dawned on me to go to Penn Station to try to get a train to New Jersey. We walked all the way from downtown up to Penn Station and the Port Authority, but nothing was running. Then we noticed an officer talking into his police radio, and by the grace of God, we overheard him say: "The boats are moving." We approached him, and he pointed us in the direction of the water.

There was only one problem, I told Penny. "I don't go on boats." It's not the boats I'm afraid of – it's the motion sickness. I've always gotten so sick on every boat I've ever been on, and I've been on a catamaran, large boats, smaller boats. Penny pointed out that this was the only way out.

When we arrived at the pier, thousands of people were waiting in line, thousands. Yet, you could hear a pin drop. That was the scariest part about it.

Penny and I walked blocks and blocks, trying in vain to find the end of the line. Eventually, we saw an opening in the line and darted in. The wait lasted three hours. Penny encouraged me because it was really weighing on my mind whether to get on this boat. And it was frustrating me because I knew I had to do it. When I finally boarded, I felt I was on my way to safety.

Most of the passengers apparently were coming from their jobs in the World Trade towers. Their clothing was covered with dust; it was on their shoes, in their hair. They were mostly younger people, but there were some older people and pregnant women. And tourists, with cameras and maps.

I sat in a corner and held on to a bolted-down chair. I stayed on the outer deck so I could feel the wind; I didn't want to feel closed in, like I was on the train. I felt a little queasy, but I knew that the worst thing now would be to get sick on this boat. So I talked myself out of getting ill, trying to focus on my ultimate goal – home.

But I couldn't shake the mental image of all those people who died in the World Trade Center. And all sorts of scenarios ran through my mind. What are the terrorists going to attack next? The boats? A suicide bomber in this crowd could've taken out thousands. The boat ride was a blessing; it saved me. But the trip across the river seemed to last hours.

It took a boat, a bus, and several trains to get me home, along with all the walking. I didn't get home until late in evening.

My manager, Patrice Hall, is transferring, and as her

last hurrah with our team, she wants us to take a lunchtime cruise around the Statue of Liberty. I love this woman; there is nothing I wouldn't do for her. And if this is the way she wants to celebrate, I'm going on that boat.

Bert Szostak:

Bert Szostak, Equity Broke
100 Wall Stree

Around 8:48, I was at the coffee vendor outside my building. I had been in the elevator when the first plane

crashed, but nothing was on the news yet. We noticed smoke coming down Wall Street, high in the air with little sheets of paper mixed in. My IT guy told me a plane just hit the Towers. I said, "Let's go take a look," thinking I'd see the tail of a Piper Cub sticking out a window.

From Liberty Park, we could see four floors of the North Tower were on fire. When two people jumped out, I said, "We have to get out of here!" Just then, we heard the engine roar of the second plane. We ducked into a cubby hole in the Century 21 building to escape the falling shrapnel. Then I ran to my building to call my wife but couldn't reach her. I called my mother and told her to tell my wife I'm okay.

Outside my building, I saw my buddy, Sean. It was literally just 5 or 10 minutes after the second crash. We were right next to Pier 11, the Wall Street Ferry port. We reached the dock around 9:30. There was a little pushing and shoving.

People began to panic and started walking down the aluminum ramps. The ramps looked as though they might collapse, and one guy handled crowd control. I said, "Screw this," and Sean and I walked right down.

A blue New York Waterway ferryboat was there, about half full, and we got on, not caring where it would take us. As crazy as it was, there were people waiting for their particular ferry.

By then, Water Street was filled with tens of thousands of people running to the Staten Island Ferry, just like in the movies. Our captain said, "Throw out the lines. We're getting out of here!" There were very few other ferryboats in the water at the time. The boat was great, and our captain was tremendous.

Not two minutes after pulling out of port, Pier 11 was engulfed in dust from the monster cloud of smoke coming down Wall Street. We thought the New York Stock Exchange had blown up. About five minutes later we rounded the tip of Manhattan. Our whole lives we've seen the towers – and then all of a sudden, one's gone. Women were screaming and crying. At this moment, someone's cell phone rang, and we learned the Pentagon had just gotten bombed. A moment later, a fighter jet zoomed overhead.

There were three passengers of Arab descent who had backpacks, and people – just average people, not police officers – demanded to know what was in those backpacks. The guys looked scared and opened their backpacks. Inside were just books. It was a real quick incident, but I noted it.

From the middle of the Hudson, we could see that the North Tower was still raging in flames. It looked like an atomic bomb had hit. We all knew that if the first tower went, the second one's going. We watched 10 to 14 people jump out of the building. The captain announced for everyone to go inside the main cabin.

The ride got very, very quiet. Everyone just stared out the cabin window, but Sean and I stood by the door. I'm a boater, and my brother's a Navy captain. If I saw one of those little orange Zodiac boats, like the one that rammed into the USS Cole and exploded, I was going to jump into the river. As remote as that might seem, I had a game plan.

As we entered the slip at Weehawken, lots of camera people were on the dock. Security guys were trying to push them away. One TV guy was filming interviews because we were on the first ferry coming out of Wall Street. Then a lady screamed, and we all turned to see the second Tower coming down. A security guard was yelling at the camera guy, and the camera guy was saying, "You know, people are dying. We have to get this on the film." It was like a fighting match.

A guy from my company, who was also on our ferryboat, drove Sean and I to the mall, and Sean's brother-in-law picked us up. We got back to his house in Saddle River at 11:30 a.m.

I've worked in New York for 15 years, and by the next Monday, it was a new city. There was camaraderie – people looking at you and saying hello versus looking at the sidewalk. It's as simple as that, but it's a big change.

Carlos J. Avila:

Carlos J. Avila, CPA, Vice President of
Tax Department, WTC Tower 2

I was using the copy machine in my office on the 82nd floor of the World Trade Center Tower 2 when suddenly

there was a sound from somewhere outside, and my building trembled. Through the window, I saw a big fireball coming at our building in slow motion. I was in shock, thinking that this was my moment to die.

Then someone screamed, "Oh my God," and that made me react. We all ran to the stairs, but three people, including myself, ran back to our desks to grab things. I closed my desk drawers and took my sunglasses, cell phone, and briefcase. That took about two minutes, and by then, almost everybody had left. My two coworkers and I took the stairs to the sky lobby on the 78th floor. My coworkers headed to an office on that floor. They ultimately died.

With no idea where the stairs to the main lobby were, I took the express elevator. About 300 people were waiting for this elevator, but I'm 5 foot 8 inches tall and managed to squeeze in. When I got to the main lobby, security people made us leave.

As I was coming out of the building, I heard a lot of people screaming. I imagined that a piece of Tower One was falling on us, so I ran across the street. When I looked back, I saw people falling, or jumping from the tower. That was one of the worst moments in my life. When the second plane hit, I thought the fireball had spread to my building from Tower One. I had no idea what was happening.

There were many people outside. We all tried to run through sidewalk scaffolding and streets at the same time. I somehow made it to a subway station near City Hall and took the No. 5 train directly to Grand Central Station then transferred to the No. 7 train to the Port Authority. Racing through the terminal, I wanted to call my roommate, my family in Puerto Rico, and my 24-year-old niece to tell them I was okay. My niece, who was living with me, worked in Manhattan also, six or seven blocks from my building.

I went to my usual gate at the Port Authority, only to learn that all the tunnels were closed. I called my room-

mate from a payphone, and he suggested that I try the ferry.

I walked almost to 50th Street, then to the port on the Westside Highway. The only boat there at the time was a sightseeing boat. I was told to go to the port at 38th Street. Downtown was like World War II. In Midtown, it was like a regular business day. The contrast was bizarre. I worried about my niece, feeling like a bad uncle for not looking for her. For the first time that morning, I cried.

When I got to 38th Street, it was around 11 AM and the ferry was still taking tickets. There was a long line, but people were buying 20 or 30 tickets and giving them out. Other people were giving away bottles of water. It was nice seeing people helping each other. Soon after, they closed the ticket window and said we didn't have to pay. I had been working in New York only 18 months and had always been told that people in New York didn't care about each other. They were wrong.

On the ferry, it was more calm and quiet. A couple of people were dirty, but most weren't. Some people were in shock or crying. Those with friends were hugging, but most people were alone. I overheard a girl say that two planes had hit the World Trade Center and that it was terrorism. I thought she just wanted attention. Then I heard someone else say that both Towers had collapsed.

The ferry was very crowded, but I did get to the upper deck to look toward the Towers. I saw nothing beyond the dust clouds. I realized that what I had overheard was probably true.

On the river, I finally had time to think. I thought about how much I wanted to arrive in New Jersey, to be with my friends, to find my niece. Even though my roommate had called my family already, I wanted my mother to hear my voice. Then I remembered something I had told my family when they visited me in the beginning of 2001. I had taken them to the 104th floor skywalk of Trade Center to enjoy the excellent view. I said that if terrorists attack the United States, the Towers would be one of the first targets.

Now, having escaped from that target, I didn't even know which port I was going to, Weehawken or West New York, and I didn't really care. All I wanted was for the boat to get me out of New York. Fortunately, it left me in close to West New York, about 20 blocks from my house.

Michelle Goldman:

Michelle Goldman, Labor Attorney
One Battery Park Plaza

I took the PATH train from Jersey City into the World Trade Center on 9/11, just like I did every morn-

ing. I walked through the underground concourse and got on the N and R subway; I was only going two stops. Around 8:48, the subway stopped running. We were stopped long enough that I remember pulling out my work; I had a court hearing that morning. Finally, it started moving and took me to my stop. When I walked up the subway-station stairs and stepped outside, everybody was looking up at the World Trade Center. Someone said that an airplane had hit, and there was a fire. I looked at it for a minute then proceeded to my office on the 11th floor of One Battery Park Plaza, about six blocks south of Ground Zero.

When I reached my desk, a coworker asked if I had heard what happened. My husband called me; he could see the fire at the top of the North Tower. Then my brother called me from Morristown, New Jersey; he, too, could see the fire. While I was on the phone with my brother, the second plane hit. I remember yelling, "The whole world is shaking!" Then I heard my coworker screaming from the next office. He actually saw the second plane hit.

At that point, we basically camped out in my coworker's office. We had no TV, so we just stared out the window and listened to the news on the radio. I emailed a few people and spoke to a friend who couldn't reach her husband at the World Financial Center. Then the computer and phones stopped working. We saw the first tower start to crumple and heard a thunderous rumbling noise. When the second tower went down, we couldn't see it because the windows had clouded over, but we heard the same rumbling – and we knew.

It was totally dark, and the smell was seeping in. Some people tried to leave but came right back because the air was so thick with dust. Everybody from my firm moved to one floor that smelled the best. Cafeteria workers brought down food. We all tried to eat and continued listening to the radio.

Around 12:30, one of the partners made an execu-

tive decision that it was okay for us to leave. She grouped everybody by location: Upper East Side, Brooklyn, West Side. I went with five or six coworkers from New Jersey. We covered our faces with T-shirts and walked thru Battery Park. It was like Christmas in summer – totally white with dust everywhere. It was eerie. We walked straight through the park to the river, where a tugboat was docked. They loaded us on.

The boat seemed old and wooden. It was crowded; and there weren't many places to stand. But I had no other way to get home. I felt grateful and relieved that I didn't have to wait for a boat and so happy to be getting out of New York. Yet, it was hard to believe I was leaving this place where we'd all been holed up together.

There was a feeling of peace on the boat, knowing it was putting the Hudson between Ground Zero and us. There was no panic and little talking. Many passengers were covered with soot. My coworker and I just kept repeating, "I can't believe this, I can't believe this."

The tugboat ride was less memorable than what happened next – and this is one of my most vivid memories of that day. As we got off the boat, rescue workers formed a kind of pathway for us. They helped people who had trouble walking. They gave us Poland Spring water, food, and towels. It almost felt like reaching a finish line.

It was an incredible sign of humanity – people of all different ages reaching out like that. These amazing people, who were they? Where were they two hours earlier, and now here they were standing on this pier, comforting strangers? I had cried during the day in my office, but my emotions were even stronger then.

I walked through Jersey City until I found a street I recognized then walked home. That took about 20 minutes. My apartment building has the most spectacular view of Lower Manhattan; that's why I live there, on the 32nd floor. Now I'm reminded of 9/11 every day at home and

when I walk past a memorial in Battery Park on my way to
work. So, in a sense, I never really escaped

Ford Crull:

Ford Crull, Visual Artist
Lower Manhattan Resident

I went out to give blood around 11:30 or 12:00, but the hospital staff wasn't prepared for all

the blood donors and sent me to the Staten Island Ferry triage area.

It was pretty deserted as I walked through the dirt and dust on Wall Street. When I got to the triage, they didn't want blood, either. I was told to walk up the Westside Highway, which I thought was rather strange since I lived only one block away. Evidently, they weren't letting people go back up Broadway. Wearing a facemask someone had given me, I was directed over to the esplanade in Battery Park City.

There, the police officers literally grabbed us and threw us on to a tugboat. I said, "Listen I'm trying to get back to my place, and this is where they sent me." But they didn't want to hear it. I think they were in shock, too. Everything was happening so fast; it was pretty disorganized. I was trying to get back home; my cats were there, and I didn't want to be stuck over in Jersey City. Perhaps it's instinct, but even amid all the turmoil, home seemed like the best place to be.

Lots of people were coming down from Battery Park City, and the police were grabbing everybody and putting them on the tugboat. One woman came with eight dogs, and they literally threw her and the dogs onto the tug. She was shrieking hysterically. The police were fairly aggressive at this point.

Part of the problem was that the boat had pulled up alongside the dock, and it was quite a drop from the dock to the boat – perhaps five feet. There was no ladder, so it could've been a little dangerous for some people. It appeared that a few people did get a little banged up. It's nobody's fault, really, but in the confusion, things got pretty hairy.

Everyone was confined to the deck area. There were 40 or 50 of us onboard, including a few children. Most were from Battery Park City; some had escaped from the Twin Towers. Everyone was subdued and upset. One guy,

who had been on the 65th floor of one of the Towers, said he'd seen a woman on fire running and jumping right out the window. He really saw the whole thing.

Some passengers worried about being left high and dry. Their concerns turned out to be valid. The tug dropped us in Jersey City, and from there, we were on our own. We asked the Jersey City police where we were supposed to go or what we were supposed to do. They didn't know. We couldn't get any information.

Finally, I walked a few miles to the PATH train. Nothing was going south, but two or three trains were going to 33rd Street, so I took one. It was around 6 p.m. when I got back to the city. I managed to walk back to my place – I sort of snuck back.

That night, I went down to the pile to help out, and I pretty much worked there the whole week. This is my neighborhood. I love it, and I wanted to be here to do whatever I could to help.

Sharlene Tobin:

Sharlene Tobin, Financial Consultant, One New York Plaza with boyfriend Matt Cronin

My boyfriend Matt and I shared an apartment about 100 yards from the South Tower. Matt was still

home around 8:40 AM when he called me at work to ask if I'd just heard a huge bang. He told me that blood was splattered all over our patio.

Around the same time, my coworker heard from his girlfriend, who worked in the World Trade Center, that an airplane crashed into the North Tower.

I was really nervous. Everyone on my floor ran to the north side of our building and saw the Towers on fire and the second plane fly by. Our building shook as the plane hit. I called Matt, and he said he was going to his office, a few blocks from the Trade Center.

My office building was being evacuated. We grabbed cell phones and handbags and took off down the stairs. I was terrified that a plane was going to hit our building. I worried about Matt's safety. To keep my mind occupied as I descended the 47 flights of stairs, I thought about joining the Marines to get revenge on whoever did this. Subconsciously, I must have understood that this was no accident.

Outside, thousands of people were standing in the street, like zombies, not knowing what to do. I ran home. My doorman said Matt had just left. We must've passed each other on the street, which was very frustrating.

I went to Matt's office and waited outside his building in case he was looking for me. But after a half hour, I entered the lobby and called his extension. He answered the phone. When I got to his floor, people were going about their normal routine. They probably didn't know what else to do.

Matt and I phoned family members, leaving voicemail messages, when we learned that the Pentagon just got hit. Our entire country was under siege.

The rumbling of the first Tower collapsing sounded like a machine gun. We imagined a gunman was outside killing people. It was wild. Through the window, we saw a cloud of smoke turning everything pitch black. Every few seconds, we'd see pieces of burning paper fly up against the window.

Around 11:30 or 12, we left and headed down Wall Street, using ripped T-shirts as masks so we could breathe. We walked toward the Brooklyn Bridge. Shoes were strewn everywhere. Business cards and letterhead from the World Trade Center were visible eight or nine blocks from where they originated, testifying to the power of the impact. We couldn't tell whether our apartment building was still standing.

My sister lives in New Jersey, so we decided to find a way to get to Hoboken. We walked to the river, and at that very moment, some guy in a New York Waterway boat pulled up against the Westside Highway, right where we were standing. There was no pier or anything, but people were getting on, so we hopped on, too. The boat captain was amazing – a real godsend. We'd been looking for a boat – and there he was.

There were at least 15 people on the boat. One guy was completely covered with soot; he looked like he'd really been through the worst of it. By then, Matt and I were also sooty from having walked through Lower Manhattan after the Towers fell.

A lot of commercial and private boats were going back and forth evacuating people at that time. In fact, many of my coworkers were also rescued by boat. One coworker said she was about to jump into the water when, out of nowhere, this boat appeared, and she got on.

Crossing the river, we smelled the burnt odor and fumes. Again, we tried in vain to locate our apartment building. It seemed wrong to look back and gawk at this horrible thing that happened, but how could we not? Yet, I don't recall anybody else looking back, just forward.

It was a very silent boat trip. Soon as we got off in Hoboken, our boat, like all the others, went right back across the river. Clearly, our captain had a strong sense of

duty. I really wish I'd gotten his name so I could thank him for having the foresight to pull up to a spot where boats did not belong to transport strangers to safety. I hope he wasn't personally affected by the tragedy.

Matt and I felt so fortunate that we survived. Some of our neighbors lost loved ones. Our apartment building was still standing, but we moved out on December 1, 2001, partly because of health concerns. I'm glad we did; there are rumors that a toxic mold has started to grow in the building adjacent to our old apartment.

Gary Welz:

Gary Welz, Comedian and Math Teacher
Resident - 75 West Street

I was asleep in my apartment at 75 West Street next door to the World Financial Center when the first plane hit.

Assuming it was street construction, I didn't even get up. About 20 minutes later, the second plane flew over my building and hit Tower Two. I turned on the TV and saw it was the Trade Center, right beside me. I immediately took the elevator downstairs and watched the Towers burning from Washington Street.

I went to the roof of my building, and about 20 neighbors were already there, watching people jumping and the Towers burning. There was blood on our roof and body parts on some of the ledges and balconies. It was very gruesome.

After 10 minutes, I went to my apartment to watch the news. My wife called, and while I was still on the phone, Tower Two fell, shaking our building and blackening the windows. I hit the deck.

Then I grabbed some clothes and my laptop computer and went into the hallway, which was quickly filling with smoke. I ran down the stairs with about five neighbors and stepped out onto Washington Street into very thick, black smoke. It looked like the aftermath of a nuclear disaster, with pulverized building six inches thick on everything, and what looked like huge gray snowflakes fluttering down.

We took refuge in the basement of the police headquarters next door for about an hour. We heard rumors that Washington, Dallas, and Chicago were also hit. "Are we shooting back," I wondered. "Is this nuclear war?"

After the second Tower collapsed, the police told us to walk to the Hudson River to be evacuated by boat. When we got to the river around 11, a double-decker, open-top boat – probably a sightseeing boat – was taking on people. They put us on the boat in a very orderly way, gave us lifejackets, and told us to sit down, as though we were going on some boring excursion.

The boat was completely full, and I was surrounded by families with kids. Everyone was absolutely silent, like a team of football players taking the bus home after losing an

away game. Everyone was deep inside themselves.

From the upper deck I smelled the odor of electrical fires and heard sirens and jets. There were a bunch of boats in the water. I got a definite feeling that any boat that could was coming to New York and taking people away. It was like Dunkirk.

From the river, we could see the remains of the Towers burning – such an unforgettable sight. The plume of smoke was huge, and we had a great panoramic view of it. Having been too close to it to see what was going on, then to get that perspective from the river was really astonishing.

The boat took us to Liberty State Park in New Jersey, where volunteers handed us bottles of water, and towels to wipe off our faces. Hundreds of people were in the park, but again, it was very quiet – like a big, surreal picnic.

Fifty people were lined up to use the park's one payphone; no one's cell phone worked. After an hour, I took the light rail from Liberty State Park station to the end of that line, which I think is Hoboken. The PATH wasn't running, so I took another light rail going in the opposite direction, to Exchange Place in Jersey City, where I hoped I'd find transportation home.

I was wandering around, trying to figure out how to get into New York, when police evacuated the buildings because they thought an attack on Jersey City was imminent. As I crossed a big street, a light rail car stopped right in front of me, and people started jumping out, fearing that a bomb was in the train. I ran away, too, then noticed I no longer had the satchel containing my laptop. Realizing I had left it on the light rail, I went back to that rail car. A police officer was opening the source of the bomb scare – my satchel. "That's mine," I said, and the policeman laughed. It was a very dream-like experience on a very surreal day.

I caught a bus to the Newark train station, had the

dust sprayed off my shoes, arms, and head; and I went through triage. By now, it was about 3 PM. Around 5, I got on a train to Penn Station in New York.

I lived in my sublet on the Upper West Side for three months before moving back home on December 15.

I must confess that I've always been fascinated by predictions of nuclear war and end-of-the-world prophecies. In a certain sense, I got what I had been fantasizing about – but in a much more vivid way.

Peter Wells:

Peter Wells, Director of Buisness Development, Information Systems Company, 75 West Street

I was in my apartment two blocks south of the Twin Towers when I heard and felt a loud boom. I ran to

the roof to see huge flames and smoke pouring out the North Tower. There were pieces of the building – and pieces of human flesh – all over the roof. A few minutes later, I heard a growing roar and saw a United 767 disappear into the South Tower, causing a tremendous explosion that blew out both sides of the building.

I ran to the stairwell as debris and shards of glass cascaded down. I returned to the roof to see both Towers engulfed in flames. Then a person jumped from the North Tower, then another and another, plummeting to their deaths. I felt horrified and utterly helpless.

I ran to my apartment and turned on the TV and learned the Pentagon had also been hit. I started packing a bag to leave. I thought the end was near.

A tremendous explosion rocked my building, and a huge plume of smoke and dust raced toward my windows. I ran to the hallway for cover. Then everything went eerily quiet and dark. I had no idea that one of the 110-story Towers had collapsed.

I finished packing and headed down the stairs with some fellow residents. We felt the ground shake again and heard another tremendous boom. The other Tower had fallen.

Six inches of dust and debris covered everything outside. A few fireman, police, and residents walked around aimlessly. Fire trucks, ambulances, and police cars were overturned, burning. A partially crushed stretcher awaited paramedics who would never return.

Out of the haze a woman walked up and gave me bottled water to wash the soot out of my mouth. I went home again and stayed there a few hours, occasionally going to the roof to see what was happening. By early evening, it was time to get to my sister's house in New Jersey.

I trudged three blocks west to a spot on the Hudson River where tugboats were evacuating people to Liberty

State Park. Calm had settled over the harbor. There was a sense of normalcy on the dock. Some people were standing around joking, as people often do in a group situation. But I realized that everything I had witnessed wasn't a nightmare; it was all terribly real. Overwhelmed with sorrow, I broke down and sat sobbing on the dock.

I boarded one of the largest tugboats I've ever seen around New York. Six or eight other passengers were on board, some with bikes, one with a black Lab. Everyone had a shoulder bag or duffel.

The deck hands were professional and very sensitive to what we had just gone through. Although they obviously had been evacuating people all day long, they didn't seem fatigued, just very methodical and focused. They were extremely polite and bent over backward to help us. For example, they made sure we didn't slip when we got on to the boat because the gangway wasn't especially clean.

As we pulled away from Manhattan at twilight, my perspective changed. All I could see was this dramatic contrast between darkened buildings, a huge hole, and a massive plume of white smoke illuminated by bright halogen floodlights. If it weren't so tragic, it would've been fascinating.

During the boat ride, people were pretty low key; we weren't in the mode of swapping stories. At one point, I almost caught myself smiling. I thought I'd leave by ferry; the last boat I expected was a tugboat. I had always loved tugboats as a kid, so I walked around to see the layout. I was impressed by the enormity of all the machinery and equipment. Even the engines and smokestack were oversized.

On the New Jersey side, there were dozens of police waiting to help us off the boat. Another 50 to 75 people were loading supplies onto other boats that were headed back to New York.

I found a ride to my sister's and got to bed around

1:30 AM. The images of the day played through my mind. I imagined all sorts of changes – we'd become a less free country, more suspicious. We'd likely experience more terror. This day seemed like the opening salvo of a continuing escalation.

Tim Seto:

Tim Seto, High School Student,
Leadership High School

I was in my first period math class, at Leadership High School in Manhattan, when one of the math

teachers ran in saying the Trade Center just got hit by an airplane. We said sarcastically, "Yeah, right." But then we looked out our window and saw all the debris. Then we ran to another classroom and stared out the window at the Trade Center. People were freaked out; everyone stopped doing their work.

An announcement on our PA system said "a little freak accident" occurred and everything was fine, so we settled down somewhat. Ten minutes later, we heard this loud boom. Our building started shaking so much I almost fell off my chair. The lights started flickering, more debris started flying around outside.

I was scared. Everyone started running out of the classrooms. I fell down the stairs and broke my left foot, although I didn't realize it at the time.

Everyone started leaving, but teachers rounded up about 30 of us and sent us to the school's basement. We waited there for about 10 minutes while the principal got the chancellor's permission to let us go.

We walked toward Battery City Park, trying to stay together. There was all this debris on the ground – newspapers, ashes, and burned stuff. The Towers looked like two smoldering cigarettes pointed upward. I thought, "This can't be real." Some of my friends said people were jumping. I might have seen a couple of small things falling out of the building, but I couldn't bear to think that those things were people.

When I reached the entrance to Battery City Park, the first building started to collapse. Clouds of dust filled the air, and everything went dark. Many of us had problems breathing because the dust was so thick and dry. We covered our faces with T-shirts and kept running around, looking for a place to go.

Thunder would be the closest description of the sound that came next; it kept going for what seemed like 20 minutes. People in the park were running back and

forth, trying to get away from the sound of the second Tower collapsing.

I was trying to reorganize myself, and teachers were trying to stay with us as much as they possibly could. By chance, some friends and I bumped into a couple of teachers, who had a plan to take the ferry to Staten Island. Meanwhile, the cloud of smoke was getting bigger and bigger.

We caught the very last ferry from Battery City Park before it closed. We were very lucky. There were thousands and thousands of people on this little ferry, it seemed. Everyone was standing, trying to make room for as many people as possible. Teachers and students were scattered around the boat, on different decks.

Moments after we left New York, there was a visible difference in the air quality. We looked back at this horrible scene then looked forward to see this clear, beautiful view of Staten Island. No clouds or smoke.

Even though the boat was crowded, it wasn't loud or rowdy. Everyone was quiet, just trying to take everything in and understand what had happened. My friend and I joked around a bit, trying to ease the tension. That, plus the thought of being taken to safety, kept me calm. I think that's when I first noticed my foot was broken. It was throbbing a little more.

After arriving in Staten Island, the teachers were trying to find the students who were on the ferry. This took a good half hour. We were taken to a police station then to nearby Curtis High School, which offered us shelter until we could get home. My friends had to help me walk; they actually found a wooden cane hanging on fence somewhere and gave it to me. I really have to thank them for that.

At Curtis High, I was taken to the nurse's office and eventually to the hospital to cast my foot and get crutches. After the Verrazano Bridge reopened, my parents picked me up.

Our whole school was transferred to Fashion and Industry High School on 24th Street until September 26 because the area around our school was still unsafe.

Due to my foot injury, I didn't go back to school until October. I found out that a Spanish teacher had broken her toe during the evacuation. We thought that was kind of funny. We were going to take a picture of the two of us for the yearbook, but it never happened.

Ariel Goodman:

Ariel Goodman, Financial Consultant,
World Trade Center, Tower 1

I own a company that was located on the 87th floor of Tower 1, and I lived across the street. I was

usually in the office by 8:30 AM, but that morning I was running late, so I was at home when I heard a huge explosion. I thought a fireworks barge had blown up on the Hudson River until I looked up at the Trade Center Towers. All I could think was, "Oh my God, if I'd been there, I would have been dead!"

I was hanging out the window taking pictures when the second plane hit; I saw it slice all the way through the building and all this stuff blow out the other end. I thought, "The whole city is under attack – this is World War III!" I started running around packing up vital documents – my passport, backups of diskettes – and my two birds.

Then I heard this crash and saw the building coming down like an avalanche. I backed up into the farthest part of my apartment; the smoke, dust, and ash were so thick so I could hardly breathe, and it was pitch black.

When I finally saw a ray of light, I grabbed my birds and ran downstairs to the lobby. The front of the building was blocked by rubble, so the doorman broke through the plate-glass windows in the rear to let us escape.

I'm a sailor, so I thought of boats right away. I couldn't see them, but I could hear them going back and forth and knew they must be evacuating people. I started to run south on the Hudson River esplanade, but then the world started to shake and Tower 1 started to fall. I just curled up into a ball over my birds.

Police began herding us toward the Holocaust Museum and told us to wait there behind barricades. But people kept jumping the barricades and running toward where they thought the boats would be. I was feeling panicky because I have asthma, and it was hard to breathe. So eventually, I jumped the barricade, too, along with a bunch of my neighbors.

It was only about a block – not a long run – but with all that smoke and ash, I was huffing and puffing. I took a running leap and jumped onto a boat that was about to pull away. I was the last person on board, and I accidentally bashed the guy who tried to catch me and my bird-

cage.

The crew kept telling us to sit down and put on life-jackets. I suppose they were doing their jobs, but at the time, it really pissed me off – I kept thinking, "This is an emergency! Does it really matter if we're sitting down? Just get us out of here!"

The boat was a sightseeing boat, with a white canopy over the top deck. It was covered with ash and dust, which blew off in a cloud as soon as we started moving, making it hard to breathe again. Still, I remember feeling a sense of total relief that I was finally out of there.

During the ride, I kept trying to see my apartment building, wondering whether I'd lost my home. I knew I'd lost my office and wondered if everyone I knew at work was dead. Most of the people on the boat were really quiet, but some kids were screaming their heads off.

When we finally got to Liberty State Park in New Jersey, we found ourselves in a gigantic marina. I was so panicky that my first thought was, "I know how to sail! Let's take a boat and get far away from here!" My companions talked me out of it, fortunately.

Instead, we started walking. We were starving, and there was nowhere to go for food because people had ransacked everything. Finally, we found a pizza place that had dough but no cheese, and a watered-down sauce, so that's what we ate.

Somebody had a friend who lived nearby; he was gracious and allowed us to stay the entire night. In his apartment, I watched TV and saw for the first time what had happened; there are no words to describe my horror.

This has changed me forever. Now, I keep a packed emergency bag and an inflatable kayak in my apartment. A couple of minutes to blow up the kayak, and I'd be ready to go.

Karen Katen
Epilogue

In the early morning hours, on a day that will forever be marked in history for its loss of innocence and suffering on a massive scale, as buildings fell and an island's earth spewed smoke and ash with volcanic fury, a call for "all available boats" penetrated the chaos with unmistakable clarity.

In the hours and days, weeks and months that followed, horror gave way to grief, and grief to recovery as stories of courage, strength and human dignity surfaced throughout our nation. New Yorkers, Americans and citizens of the world instinctively reached out to each other to make certain that good would ultimately triumph over evil.

In the telling and retelling of this unparalleled maritime response, the largest spontaneous wartime evacuation by boat since Dunkirk in World War II, we will remember that when faced with the worst threat to our humanity we responded without hesitation and came ashore.

On September 11, 2001, two thousand eight hundred and twenty three lives were lost in New York City and many hundreds of thousands of lives were permanently changed. Yet on that same day, and the days that followed, in the midst of sadness and grief, we witnessed surprising strength and resilience as a people. We were wounded, but not mortally. We were paralyzed, but not permanently. We were isolated, but not for long and not from each other.

The waters still surround us carrying life as they did that day. They continue to nurture our spirits and remind us of those many acts of courage and heroism displayed without a second thought. And they gently guide us to a better place where hope displaces hate, and the calming breeze of new life softens the pain and turns us gently toward a brighter future.

Karen Katen is the president of
Pfizer Global Pharmaceuticals in New York City.

Photo Credits